COLIN WILKINSON

THE BLUECOAT PRESS

In loving memory
of Claire McKeown
1978 - 2011

Book design by Daniel Bickerton
Printed in Belgium by DeckersSnoeck

ISBN 9781908457059

Acknowledgements
This book would not have been possible
without the assistance of Getty Images
who provided all the photographs.
Particular thanks to Caroline Theakstone for
searching out many previously unpublished
photographs and Philip Grimwood-Jones for
his help in licensing their use. The icing on
the cake was provided by John Chillingworth
and Thurston Hopkins, two surviving Picture
Post photographers (Hopkins still remarkably
active at 98), who provided invaluable
information. Finally, to Liz Wilkinson for her
proofreading and constant support.

PICTURE
POST
ON LIVERPOOL

COLIN WILKINSON

THE BLUECOAT PRESS

The photograph, by Leonard McCombe, could be Liverpool but is actually Birkenhead.
It was published in July 1944 in an article about Planning Post-War Britain.

4

Introduction

Picture Post's first cover. Apparently, Edward Hulton wanted a battleship but Stefan Lorant gave him two cowgirls jumping in the air.

I was too young to remember Picture Post. When its final issued was published in 1957, I was only nine and my reading matter was Beano, Dandy and any other comic I could lay my hands on. My only contact with the world of newspapers and magazines was the daily arrival of The Times, a truly dull paper locked into its Victorian and Edwardian past, with the front page dedicated to advertising; not large corporate offerings, but hundreds of small insertions offering a bewildering array of services for the upper middle-classes.

A public school and Oxbridge-educated elite had control of the news and they dictated what the population was told, either through the medium of print or through the airwaves.

Men like Lord Reith had determined what was enlightening and that was what the population was fed. It was into this hide-bound world that an émigré Hungarian Jew escaping Nazi persecution arrived, bringing with him a new European perspective.

Stefan Lorant was a publisher in Germany and had been imprisoned by Hitler for his troubles. His magazines combined wit, insight and irreverence with strong graphics and illustration. All these elements were brought together in Picture Post and its freshness and relevance were instantly successful. Here was a magazine that succinctly explained the big issues of the time with strong picture-led stories that were rarely patronising or dull.

Two children read a comic together in the Pitt Street area. Photographed by Bert Hardy in 1940. (Not published)

A template had been created and photo-journalism in Britain found a solid foundation. Although the magazine was later to fail, largely as a result of straying away from the ethos it had established, it remains a potent symbol of what journalism can achieve at its best.

My interest in Picture Post was sparked off, as it is in so many cases, by discovering a small collection of magazines. I was running the Open Eye project in Liverpool at the time and established a photography gallery there a few years later. At the back of my mind was the idea of holding an exhibition of photographs from the magazine but I left before I could realise it. (Open Eye did, in fact, put on an excellent exhibition of Bert Hardy's Liverpool photographs a few years later).

My career took a different path, but almost 30 years on, after adding considerably to my collection, I managed to locate every issue that dealt with Liverpool.

Furthermore, the purchase of the Hulton archive by Getty Images resulted in an online presence of many of the images from the articles in which I was interested. With Getty Images' help, a whole new cache of unseen and unpublished photographs was unearthed and many of these appear here for the first time.

My aim in writing this book is not only to show the many magnificent photographs taken by photographers such as Bert Hardy, John Chillingworth and Thurston Hopkins, but also to reveal the way in which Liverpool was portrayed by Picture Post.

The most exciting part of my research was corresponding with Thurston Hopkins, still remarkably active at 98 (he apologised for taking so long to reply but he had been too busy organising an exhibition of his work, along with other business). His lengthy reply to a vexing question about censorship can be read in the final chapter. What he also added was that he still remembered the warmth of the welcome he received as he was photographing some of the worst slums in the country. It is his humanity and that of his fellow photographers that shines through on every page of this book. Here is a legacy of photographs that brilliantly captures a troubled time for Liverpool as it struggled to cope with the aftermath of War.

Professor Codman,
Liverpool's famous
Punch and Judy man.
Photographed by
Bert Hardy in 1955.
(Not published)

A Short History
of Picture Post

The famous issue of 4 January 1941 which put forward 'A Plan for Britain'. Published at a critical time for Britain, when the threat of invasion was ever-present, it put forward a bold plan for social, educational and industrial reform, later to be integrated in many aspects of the Welfare State.

I have only written a brief account of Picture Post's history. For those wishing to read about the magazine in more detail, Tom Hopkinson, editor from 1940-50, has written two splendid books: his autobiography *Of This Our Time* (Hutchinson, 1982) and *Picture Post 1938-50* (Penguin Press, 1970). Both books give vivid accounts of the launch of Picture Post, the personalities involved, and the ethos and ideology that sustained it. Two later accounts by Robert Kee (*The Picture Post Album: A 50th Anniversary Collection*) and Gavin Weightman (*Picture Post Britain*) are less detailed, but take the magazine's story through to its demise.

Magazine publishing has always been a precarious business. There are relentless deadlines, a constant pressure to find advertising and a never-ending battle to expand circulation. For every successful magazine, there are dozens that have disappeared from the news stands, some within months, but others after a protracted decline in the face of financial and readership meltdown.

There are, of course, many different kinds of publication. The specialist magazine dealing with consumer interests such as photography, cars, fashion, or sport, has a clearly targeted audience and can usually rely on advertisers who wish to reach that specific group. The best of these magazines can be highly profitable and the brand leaders are familiar in all newsagents.

The general magazine has a more difficult task. It is aimed at a very broad population and relies on a mix of articles that will, in a large part, satisfy most of its readers. The vision is of a mass circulation that will then support the highest rates of advertising to supplement the income from its consumer sales. To achieve its target, it must have content that excites and an unerring ability to keep at the cutting edge of its industry.

The rise and fall of Picture Post is a fascinating example of such a magazine. It emerged at one of the most critical times in modern history – the beginning of the Second World War. Its first issue, in October 1938, gives few clues to the impending crisis, at a time when appeasement was the official policy, but the editor, Stefan Lorant, was a Hungarian Jew who had been imprisoned by Hitler for criticising the mistreatment of Jews by the Nazis and he was only too clear as to what Germany's plans were. Lorant had fled to Britain where he continued his career in journalism by producing a successful pocket-sized magazine, Lilliput. This was the model for a new kind of magazine based on his knowledge of the European market. It was to be photographically based, with picture stories rather than the usual hard blocks of text with occasional illustrations. It was to mix politics and current affairs with articles about people and places, with clear and uncomplicated journalism.

Fortuitously, Edward Hulton, an ex-Harrovian and son of a newspaper magnate, was looking to build his own media empire. Lorant persuaded Hulton to invest in a new magazine, and with Hulton's money behind him, Picture Post was born.

In the staid world of publishing at that time, Picture Post was a revelation, exceeding its circulation target from the first week. Under inspired editorial control, the best available photographers, journalists and contributors were recruited, and between them they created a legendary magazine that set the standard in Britain. Its familiar red and white masthead was instantly recognisable, as were its punchy graphics and attractive layout.

When Lorant departed to America in 1940, in the belief that Britain would fall to the Nazis, his more than able deputy Tom Hopkinson took over and, under his leadership, the magazine became not just a voice of the people but also its conscience. Its regular features were not just about morale-boosting but also about planning for the future, concentrating on the values the country was fighting to preserve. The Beveridge Report on the Welfare State owed much to the groundwork laid down by Picture Post in features such as A Plan for Britain, in 1941, in which a whole raft of reforms was suggested and later adopted by Atlee's Post-War Labour government.

In the austerity years that followed the War, Picture Post still maintained its circulation, but problems began to surface over the involvement of its proprietor. Edward Hulton, although a Conservative, had largely supported the ideas behind the Welfare State. He believed in a more equitable society and was somewhat at odds with the majority in his party in his strongly pro-European views. However, he rapidly became disillusioned with the Labour Government and this brought him into conflict with editor Tom Hopkinson. In 1950, matters came to a head over a story written by James Cameron (with photographs by Bert Hardy) on the mistreatment of Communist prisoners of war by the South Koreans. Hopkinson realised the story was dynamite and asked Cameron to tone his article down to avoid over-sensationalism. Hulton, however, asked for the feature to be withdrawn and when he refused, Hopkinson was sacked.

From that point onwards, the magazine's days were numbered. Rejection of its core values was compounded by Hulton regularly changing editors, even taking over the role himself for a time. Outwardly, Picture Post seemed to be the same magazine. Editorship passed on to Hopkinson's deputy, the able Ted Castle, but within a few months his Labour stance had annoyed Hulton and his contract was terminated. The art department still retained its key personnel and there was no obvious change to the high quality of its layout. Additionally, many of the best photographers continued to work for the magazine and exciting new writers were recruited. Changes were taking place, though, from an increase in its glamour content to

Another 1940 Bert Hardy photograph of children eating apples as they read a comic outside a shop. (Not published)

a disastrous increase in its cover price (to 6 pence but then lowered back to 4 pence). Advertising was allowed to appear, aping Picture Post layouts, something Hopkinson would never have allowed.

Increasingly, the tone of the magazine became patronising as Hulton lost sight of who his audience was. The advent of television compounded the magazine's problems as circulation slumped.

No longer at the cutting edge, Picture Post had lost the originality and freshness that had served it so well in its earlier years. Now it was just another magazine with dreary articles about film stars, fashion and society gossip. The occasional harder-hitting piece of photo-journalism seemed lost amongst such a mediocre mix.

The final issue was released on 1 June 1957, with the same picture of two girls that appeared on its first cover. Hulton blamed television for its demise but the truth was that it had lost its audience for other reasons. Photo-journalism thrived in other countries: Life magazine and Paris-Match are two examples of magazines that have continued to prosper. In Britain, there was nothing to take its place. Fortunately, history has been kind to Picture Post. It is still seen as a beacon of excellence and talked about by many who were too young to have read it during its 20-year lifetime. That, in itself, is a fine accolade.

Liverpool waterfront, 1954. A moody picture by Bert Hardy, one of a planned series about Liverpool transport. (Not published)

Liverpool and Picture Post

Within months of its launch in 1938, almost the sole focus of Picture Post was to cover the War in a meaningful and informative way. There were severe restrictions of what could be published and every article had to be passed by the Official Censor. Anything that could be interpreted as being of benefit to the enemy was likely to be rejected, although this had to be a sensitive process: the public needed to be informed and this often included bad news.

One of the hardest hitting features was titled 'Back to the Middle Ages', with dramatic photographs illustrating the evils of Nazism. Tom Hopkinson wrote later that such pages 'are propaganda – and propaganda is often taken to be a dirty word. But propaganda is noble or degrading according to the cause it supports, the emotions it appeals to, and the methods it employs.'

In this context, the Blitz on London was covered prominently, projecting the spirit of the brave East Enders carrying on day after day in the face of appalling bombing. With the exception of a feature on the desecration of Coventry's cathedral and medieval heart, little was written about the devastating attacks on other places such as Liverpool, which suffered the highest rate of casualties per capita of any city. Possibly that was due to the Censor wishing to keep a tight lid on information about strategic damage to ports and industrial sites. It might also reflect an editorial decision to keep its stretched staff in London, where there was plenty of action to report on. Whatever the reasons, the one-sided coverage by the media in general created a mythology that only London suffered in the Blitz, a viewpoint that still survives 70 years on.

In fact, the first article concerning Liverpool was in July 1941. There had been an earlier piece on the tragedy of HMS Thetis but that was in Liverpool Bay and the city was incidental to the article. The highly respected writer JB Priestley travelled to Liverpool to investigate 'The Truth about the Dockers' in response to a widely held view that dockers (nationally, although the article focused on Liverpool) were hindering the flow of supplies through the port. In an even-handed response, Priestley discovered a failure of the port authorities to provide adequate canteen facilities for men, mainly dockers too old for conscription, who were mentally and physically exhausted carrying out dirty and dangerous work under the stress of air-raids, and who lacked necessary hot meals to sustain them. Taking a swipe at any armchair critics, he asked how many of them were capable of working a docker's week.

The problem arises, notwithstanding such a strong rebuttal, that insidious damage was being caused to Liverpool's standing. Mud had been thrown and some of it stuck. The Liverpool docker had been castigated as unpatriotic and truculent and a stereotype had been created in the minds of the public.

Quite remarkably, nothing further was written about Liverpool until March 1949. There were occasional pieces about the Grand National but they were about horses, trainers and owners and have no relevance to this book. There was also a feature, in August 1941, about planning the future of Britain, which focused on Liverpool University's School of Architecture but that is about issues not specifically related to the city. The article on the Rodney Youth Club was the first specific feature on Liverpool. Once again, the over-riding tone is sympathetic and it is perhaps harsh to criticise the well-meant, but clearly middle-class values of journalist John Ormond Thomas from a distance of over sixty years. Putting such sentiments on one side, the Liverpool slums had become the story. Dirty-faced kids in worn-out clothes abandoned by their parents on the streets; dreary streets with run-down housing; unemployment and despair. This could not be Oxford, Cambridge, Bath or London, it could only be Liverpool. All the journalist had to do was board a train to Lime Street and take a five minute walk up Mount Pleasant and there was his story. Within weeks, in July 1949, another article was published about the 'Colour Bar'. It is incredible to read that there were only 25,000 'coloured' people in Britain at that time, with some 8,000 living in Liverpool. The issues facing the Afro-Caribbean population were of housing and job discrimination and cultural alienation, problems that would multiply with time. It is an important feature written by a young Robert Kee and illustrated by Bert Hardy's dramatic photographs, taken, in the main, on the streets of Liverpool 8. This was not easy journalism, there was a wave of racial tension in London and elsewhere, but again a negative image is portrayed of Liverpool – the city of slums.

An article on Liverpool Football Club's unsuccessful trip to Wembley in 1950 is, like the Grand National features, of little interest. The Cup Final nearly always featured and the usual journalistic laziness in summarising the possible outcome (it could go either way) are no more than one would expect.

Four years later and a series 'The Best and Worst of British Cities' started with Liverpool, although one might struggle to pinpoint what was the best on offer; hardly a mention of culture, sport or great architecture; just a rather sad piece on the decline of a once-great port. In its own words: 'This is, at best, a sketch. The essence of Liverpool is not easily distilled. It has a sad look of glory gone to seed.'

That was in April, 1954, and in November, reporter Brian Dowling and Bert Hardy made the trip North to shadow the larger-than-life Bessie Braddock, once a Communist firebrand but now one of the prominent figures in the Labour party. 'Battling Bessie' was the bête noire of the right wing press, everything they hated most – a straight-talking Socialist who also happened to be a Catholic, a woman and from Liverpool. Once again, the article was complimentary but this was the fourth successive main feature that had appeared in five years and all had concerned themselves with the problems of the slums and economic decline. It is hardly surprising that a fortnight later Brian Dowling and Bert Hardy's article on 'A Boy's Best Friend is a Policeman' tackled Liverpool's juvenile crime and the police's innovative response.

Dowling and Hardy used their time in Liverpool productively. An article in December about the football pools included a brief description of the Littlewoods' empire (with photographs taken by Haywood Magee) of its Liverpool operation and on Christmas Day, 1954, the first really positive article appeared on the Shakespeare Theatre, one of the grandest surviving variety theatres in Britain. The theatre was struggling and the sense of glory days long gone pervades the feature.

The building of Liverpool Cathedral was the subject of an effusive piece in June 1955:

The cathedral is the finest and the greatest built in Britain since Henry VIII destroyed the monasteries. Almost certainly, it will be the last great Anglican cathedral. The cathedral, built to last at least two thousand years, puts to shame those who have said the time for building great churches is long since past.

Any thought that Picture Post had gone soft on Liverpool was completely dispelled by two final features that examined the phenomenon of the teenager: 'The young people who suck sticky brown stuff through straws, stay out too late, wear the wrong clothes, and think they know it all.'

The first part, published in March 1957 has, as its first photograph, a young man lounging on his bed. The caption reads: 'A teenager going nowhere: one of Liverpool's unemployed youths sits out another day.' Facing is a photograph of earnest pupils listening to a debate at Great Barr comprehensive school in Birmingham. Journalist Trevor Philpott effuses about how the school is motivating its pupils and how the community is involved and caring. Turn the page and the tone changes:

But come to Liverpool where things are rather different, and meet Harry. He's on probation. He is 16 and unemployed… His home is enough to make your throat shrink with pity and disgust. On the morning we went there his mother was in. "I've got no 'eart to do anything anymore. No 'eart to do anything." It is gruesomely obvious.

December 1955, and Liverpudlians enjoy a final drink together to say farewell to friends and family before embarking on their journey west to Canada. Photograph by Jack Smith. (Not published)

The sadness is that Liverpool had many fine schools at the time that were the equal or more of Great Barr but that would have spoiled the story. Perhaps the giveaway is the line which exposes the journalist's background and values: 'And the third (place he visited) was where most teenagers would like the chance to live – in Cambridge University.' Could it get any worse? Part two the following week made sure it did. A double page photograph shows two young men grabbing at a girl on a dark street corner. The caption: 'Boys meet girls in a Liverpool street. Yes, the social graces have changed a little. No time now for many of the formalities of courtship.' The article is not about 'The Truth about Teenagers', for there is no balance here. It is about Everton Boys Club and sub-titled 'Boys without a Future'. It is about stealing cars, hanging-out in coffee bars and dance-halls in West Derby Road and girls. 'Sooner or later the boys will find themselves with time on their hands, a dark place - and her.'

In the final episode, Picture Post looked at 'Those Wild, Wild Girls' but there was no wildness shown, just polite girls in a mill canteen, Cambridge students walking through college cloisters and singing on the banks of the

River Cam. The talk is of university, careers and the future… no mention of unemployment, thieving or Liverpool.

There were no further articles about Liverpool. A few weeks after 'The Truth about Teenagers', Picture Post died. Its last issue on 1 June 1957 drew the final curtain on what had been an innovative and often brilliant magazine. The perspective of this book has been to examine its relationship with Liverpool and it is disappointing that it was in part responsible for the demonising of a city struggling with deep problems of urban decay. It chose to ignore the many positive qualities of a great seaport and contributed towards the media obsession with Liverpool – the problem city. As a final thought, a feature 'Is Talent Inherited?', in January 1948, concluded:

It is doubtful whether Beethoven could have become the genius he did had he been born 20 years ago in a Liverpool slum. A child's sensibilities are sharpened or dulled by what goes on around it.

One cannot argue with that basic premise but, 15 years later, four working-class lads shook the world and every young person wanted to be from Liverpool.

The Photographers

The three key photographers whose work is represented in this book are John Chillingworth, Godfrey Thurston Hopkins and Bert Hardy. They each had a distinctive style and Liverpool is fortunate that their images have survived as a brilliant portrayal of the city in the 1940s and 50s.

John Chillingworth (1928 -)

John Chillingworth was, in one sense, born into the world of newspapers. His father was a senior union official in Fleet Street and John was able to gain the opportunity to assist staff photographers on their assignments. Having served as an army photographer towards the end of the War, he joined Picture Post in 1949 and gained invaluable experience from Kurt Hutton, one of the magazine's greatest photographers. Between 1949 and 1956, he photographed over 400 assignments for Picture Post, including his essay on Liverpool: 'The Best and Worst of British Cities'.

Bert Hardy (1913 - 1995).

London born, he left school at 14 to work for a chemist who processed photographs. Deciding photography was for him, he started freelancing for The Bicycle magazine, saving enough money to buy a Leica 35mm camera. In 1941, Tom Hopkinson recruited Hardy as a staff photographer, rising to become Chief Photographer. He had an active war, photographing the Blitz, D-Day landings and the liberation of Belsen concentration camp amongst many assignments. With James Cameron, he covered the Korean War, taking the controversial photographs of the mistreatment of Communist prisoners that led to the sacking of Tom Hopkinson over Edward Hulton's

stance over their publication. Famously, he wrote that photographers did not need an expensive camera to take a good picture and proved it with his iconic picture of two girls sitting on railings at Blackpool taken on a Box Brownie. His work in Liverpool was substantial, from Chinese seamen in 1942 (not published), the city's black community (published in 1950) as well as unpublished projects on Lime Street station, the ferries, carters and other subjects that caught his attention.

Godfrey Thurston Hopkins (1913 -)

Thurston Hopkins' father was a prolific author, who wrote about a wide range of subjects from ghosts, industrial archaeology and the English countryside to biographies of Oscar Wilde, HG Wells and Kipling. Thurston attended Brighton College of Art, training to be an illustrator but converted to photography as a career because it offered a more reliable living.

During the War, he served with the RAF Photographic Unit and, after being demobbed, continued as a freelancer, eventually joining Picture Post in 1949 and becoming a full member of staff in 1951. His one assignment in Liverpool was to take photographs for the proposed 'Slums of Liverpool' feature discussed in the final chapter.

A desolate, misty street captured by Thurston Hopkins. (Not published)

In a detailed response, John Chillingworth indicates, the role of the photographers in Picture Post was of paramount importance and they had a significant role in deciding magazine content.

Throughout the Picture Post era, editor's Monday morning meeting demanded that all available staff photographer, journalists and department heads attended. Each one of those attending was expected to speak, presenting one or more picture story ideas for the editor's consideration. In the ten years of Tom Hopkinson's editorship, the photographers were more important than journalists; it being a picture magazine, the journalist's primary task was to ensure that the photographer got his pictures. The copy could be worked upon after the assignment.

Each individual staff photographer had very little knowledge of the way in which colleagues worked. If Godfrey Thurston Hopkins worked alone, that is something of a surprise to me. Nevertheless, the quality of his results spoke for themselves. Hayward Magee very often worked alone, because he was as brilliant a writer as he was a photographer. Bert Hardy certainly had a journalist with him, sometimes acting a facilitator, at others as a caption writer, before drafting copy at a late date, but when he worked on major assignments,

particularly abroad, he and the writer were invariably a close team. That is certainly the way in which I worked.

In all probability, Bert would have worked in Liverpool with a journalist, initially upon assignments agreed by the editor and subsequently on ideas that may have presented themselves at the time. It would be true to say that a percentage of stories shot by every photographer, did not reach the pages of the magazine, due largely to the fast-moving nature of weekly magazines.

There was no distinction between staff photographers and staff journalists. Status was not an issue and an Oxbridge background cut little ice with editors; what they were hiring was experienced journalists, whatever their background. When my colleagues and I worked with freelance writers whose perception of the photographer/journalist relationship was different to the Picture Post teamwork ethos, they were rapidly disabused of their error and harmony reigned. The one exception was when we worked with MP's seeking to supplement their income. Some had delusions about their own importance. When the facts of Picture Post life were imparted and they still could not stomach the teamwork principle, the editor would explain the gravity of their error and expect them to conform.

Grim-faced dockers queue up to receive their week's pay,
Photographed for the article but not published.

The Truth about the Dockers

With American aid we shall win this war. American aid comes to us through the docks. Does it come through them fast enough? Could it come faster? Priestley goes North to find out.

Published 26 July 1941. Text by J B Priestley.

The first article to appear in Picture Post specifically about Liverpool was published in July 1941. The subject matter was not the devastation wreaked on the city by night after night of enemy bombing, nor was it the heroics of the seamen engaged in the deadly Atlantic convoys. It was, instead, a piece by JB Priestley, about whether dockers in Liverpool and Manchester were pulling their weight in the fight against Nazism. The sub-title spells out the problem – clearly the subject had become the focus of attention because otherwise Picture Post would not have covered it. In a well-balanced article, the case is laid out:

When I arrived in Liverpool, I had in my bag two extremely interesting documents. Nothing could better illustrate the difficulty of this dockers' problem than a comparison of these two documents. One of them was a copy of a letter from a big shipping firm. It was complaining about the new Dock Labour Scheme, under which every registered docker, so long as he reports for work, receives a guaranteed minimum of £4 2s 6d a week. He may, of course, earn considerably more than this if he is actually being employed all week. But the writer complained that the scheme was encouraging most of the men to slack, which they did by dodging the foremen who had to pick the teams for unloading.

The other document was a copy of a report from a Ministry of Food official, which declared that a certain class of cargo, of vital importance to the country, had been discharged in record time. "I think it would be appropriate," he concludes, "if the dockers were congratulated on the efforts they have made. If they keep this up (and of course, they must slow off in the dark nights) they will have earned the gratitude of the country, and to tell them so properly will encourage them to greater efforts."

Well, there you are, two contradictory reports, one accusing most of the men of deliberately slacking, the other testifying to their recent efforts. In addition, one has read, of course, various conflicting statements in the Press. What was the truth? On the whole the docker is well satisfied with what he earns. This varies considerably, now that he is on piece-work, but the average is probably round about six pounds a week. Some earn less. A few earn more, but these as a rule have not only been working overtime but have also been engaged for special jobs, such as unloading damaged cargoes from ships that have been bombed. This work can be dangerous as well as hard. In some circumstances it can be very tough going indeed, and armchair critics of the dockers, who found themselves having to put in nine or ten hours of such work, might soon change their minds.

It has been suggested in some quarters that dockers as a class care little about the war effort, feel themselves detached from it, and only want to exploit the national emergency to improve their own conditions. So far as I could gather, this applies to only a small proportion of the Merseyside dockers. After all, most of the men have sons or brothers in the services or the mercantile marine. Moreover, it is the dockers and their families everywhere who have felt the full weight of Nazi bombing at its most ruthless pitch. It is they who have been in the front line here. It is not necessary to tell them that "there's a war on", for they know all about that, having seen plenty of it. Therefore this is not a case where special propaganda is necessary.

There are many reasons, quite apart from faulty organisation and enemy bombing, why output should have gone down in this area. Thus, a great many young dockers in Liverpool, where before the war less than fifty percent of its twenty thousand dockers were in regular employment, left to join the services. This meant that when the port was being used to capacity, older men were called upon to do the work. Again, before the war Liverpool docks had specialised in certain classes of cargo, cotton and the like, which could be discharged with the minimum of delay. But when general cargoes of all kinds had to be discharged at these same docks, there was necessarily some delay, and so output of clearance went down. I mention this if only to show how misleading mere figures may be if all facts are not taken into consideration.

Picture Post,
July 26, 1941

HEROES OR LOAFERS ? *Liverpool Dockers Ready to Go Off to a Job*
Work or no work, dockers must report each day at the control point. Work or no work, they earn a wage. These men
have reported. There is work for them. An official takes their names before they go off on the job.

The Truth about the Dockers
by J. B. Priestley

With American aid we shall win this war. American aid comes to us through the docks. Does it come
through them fast enough ? Could it come faster ? Priestley goes North to find out.

IT was decided that we should visit Liverpool and Manchester, to photograph and write about the dockers. This needed the co-operation of two authorities: the Admiralty, which readily gave permission, and the Port Controller, Mr. Gibson Jarvie. The latter announced that he was not prepared to co-operate with us or give us any facilities on the docks. (This was an attitude quite new to me, for I have always found officials of every kind eager to co-operate.) Therefore it must be understood that what follows represents my own private opinions. Mr. Gibson Jarvie does not come into it at all.

When I arrived in Liverpool, I had in my bag two extremely interesting documents. Nothing could better illustrate the difficulty of this dockers'

problem than a comparison of these two documents. One of them was a copy of a letter from a big shipping firm. It was complaining about the new Dock Labour Scheme, under which every registered docker, so long as he reports for work, receives a guaranteed minimum of £4 2s. 6d. a week. He may, of course, earn considerably more than this if he is actually being employed all week. But the writer complained that the scheme was encouraging most of the men to slack, which they did by dodging the foremen who had to pick the teams for unloading.

The other document was a copy of a report from a Ministry of Food official, who declared that a certain class of cargo, of vital importance to the country, had recently been discharged in record

time. " I think it would be appropriate," he concludes, " if the dockers were congratulated on the efforts they have made. If they keep this up (and of course, they must slow off in the dark nights) they will have earned the gratitude of the country, and to tell them so properly will encourage them to greater efforts."

Well, there you are. Two contradictory reports, one accusing most of the men of deliberately slacking, the other testifying to their recent efforts. In addition, one had read, of course, various conflicting statements in the Press. What was the truth ? That is what I had to try and discover for myself.

On the whole the docker is well satisfied with what he earns. This varies considerably, now that

23

THE WORK OF THE DOCKERS: *Unloading at the Docks*

At the Local Dockers' Conferences Dockyard Grievances Are Thrashed Out
Dockers have genuine grievances. Not about pay, facilities, transport facilities, housing accommodation. J. B. Priestley sits in at a conference.

Work on the Docks is Usually Heavy, Often Dangerous

What the Dockers' Work Means to the War Effort
Aeroplanes—most vital import from the U.S.A.—come ready assembled out of the holds of ships on to Liverpool's massive open-ended docks. Cranes that can handle 200 tons at a time lay them delicately in position. Drawn by lorries, they roll off in convoy to nearby aerodromes.

One of the main focuses of Priestley's article was the failure of the authorities to provide proper canteen facilities for its workers. In peacetime, most dockers could rely on one hot meal a day at home, but the catastrophic bombing had disrupted such daily routines. They were really in the position of front line troops in an army that had no Quartermaster's department at all. Any general asked to lead troops under such conditions would probably resign at once. The men were ready and willing to work, but what they asked for, reasonably enough, were facilities to enable them to do the work. If you are uncertain where you may sleep next, have not had a substantial hot meal for days, and find that it takes weary hours to get to and from your work, then you are going to complain. And you will not unreasonably be annoyed if you are told that because you complain, you are merely taking advantage of the national emergency and you are unpatriotic. Clearly influenced by what he experienced in Liverpool, Priestley fires off a final salvo:

Let there be no more grumbling about the dockers, especially from people who could not lead a docker's life for a week; but instead a recognition of the fact that, apart from a handful of dodgers and professional malcontents, the dockers are doing their vital jobs as best they can.

An interesting postscript to the feature was the subject of Picture Post's editorial of 10 August 1941. Mr J Gibson Jarvie, Regional Port Director of the North-Western Area, had written a strong letter condemning the magazine's decision to publish the article on the basis that he had refused to grant press facilities for journalist JB Priestley (and the photographer) without the finished article being submitted for approval. Picture Post addressed his complaint with a pithy: 'Picture Post recognises the established and necessary censorship set up by the Government. It does not, and will not, recognise the right of officials to set themselves up as private censors over their own provinces.'

Surprisingly, Picture Post did
not use this photograph of a
policeman pointing the way to
the Youth Club.

The only other Saturday playground. A bomb-site in a mean street near Rodney Youth Centre. Until the Centre opens in the afternoon, the children taste play as it always was before the Club began. (Picture Post caption)

The Street Corner with a Roof On

'The street corner with a roof on': that's what they call the Rodney Youth Centre. Inside, some of Liverpool's toughest and poorest 'dead-end kids' find a substitute for normal organised club life.

Published 5 March 1949
Text by John Ormond Thomas
Photographed by Charles Hewitt

Above the article heading, a photograph of a young boy holding hands with his much younger sister catches the eye. Their anxiety is palpable, maybe because, as the caption unwittingly reveals, 'He gets his first sight of swings, football and fighting with gloves on.' On the same page are two other photographs; one of 'a bomb-site in a mean street near the Rodney Youth Centre. Until the Centre opens in the afternoon the children taste play as it always was before the Club began' and the other of 'The Luxury of

The poor boy looks terrified as his friends encourage him to take further punishment. (Not published)

a Mat for Wrestling" ('No scrambling on the muddy bomb-sites. Here a boy can strip down and have a proper bout.'). The feature is of particular interest because, with its images of poorly dressed, grubby faced kids, it is one of the first photo-journalistic examples of Liverpool becoming the target of London-based media looking to highlight the broader national problem of urban deprivation. The Youth Centre was housed at the Wellington Buildings, in Mount Pleasant, later to become The Irish Centre and currently vacant. A splendid Georgian building that had once been a ballroom for Liverpool's high society, its better days were long behind it by 1949. After a difficult start, the Centre had appointed Stella Baker as Warden and it was her commitment and organisation that had drawn national attention to the project. The activities ranged from the artistic (puppet theatres, painting, tap dancing and singing) to the occupational (seamanship, woodwork and shoe-repairing) to dancing and sport (including boxing, wrestling and indoor rugby). John Ormond Thomas, the journalist, was clearly impressed:

In quiet ways the place has grown more orderly, and the children who, when I first met them, were wild or shy to the point of tears on being talked to by a stranger, have grown well-mannered and easy in conversation.

The club has inspired confidence in very many: boys have grown to feel they are as good as the next, though the seats of their trousers are out. The football team, for instance, has joined a local league and lost only one game this season; the club provides the kit, and not a single jersey or stocking has been lost. Five years ago every one would have been missing inside a week.

Unfortunately, the tone always falls on the side of condescension. Expressions such as 'boys have grown to feel they are as good as the next, though the seats of their trousers are out' and 'five years ago every one would have been missing inside a week' are echoed in the concluding paragraph:

Children are being cared for and encouraged in ways which will lead them to use their leisure in a decent fashion. They are being given a chance to know something better than the playground of the streets. They are learning to 'fit in'.

What is a 'decent fashion' and fitting in to what, one might ask? A magazine largely run by public school and university educated journalists clearly had its own ideas.

(Opposite) A new member is introduced to the Centre. He hasn't been inside the doors of Rodney Youth Centre before. He gets his first sight of swings and fighting with gloves on. (Picture Post caption)

(Top) The seniors take over for dancing. There are some excellent jitterbugs. The Chief Constable of Liverpool is a Rodney supporter and warmly approves its work. (Picture Post caption)

(Left) The footballer takes a half-time breather. He's had enough for the moment, so he's called half-time. And as long as he keeps his foot on the ball, it'll continue to be half-time. (Picture Post caption)

(Left) Club members of Rodney: Swing Fan. If you haven't seen a swing before, you're careful. But, with friends to help, it doesn't take long to make you an enthusiast. (Picture Post caption)

(Bottom) Unwillingly, wishing there were no such things as clocks or beds or turning-out times, the children leave for home. But they'll be back tomorrow night. They'll be at the front door of the Club an hour before it's due to open. There'll be kicks and hammerings at it, which won't stop until it swings open to let them rush in again from the dark streets to their playing paradise. (Picture Post caption)

(Right) A gentleman takes his ease. Racing a rubber-tyre can be hard work. And at Rodney, you can race about as long as you like. When you've got your breath back, you can start again.
(Picture Post caption)

A young family enjoying the sunshine. (Not published)

Is There a British Colour Bar?

Published 2 July 1949
Written by Robert Kee
Photographed by Bert Hardy

The striking magazine cover of the Colour Bar article.

The feature article in1949, tackled that most persistent and difficult subject – racism. Today, the use of the word 'coloured' is offensive and has been replaced by more appropriate definitions but it was the accepted appellation at the time of the article, along with the word Negro. The real focus of the story is not crude outmoded racial terminology, but the astonishingly disproportionate reaction to the presence of such a small immigrant population. The opening paragraph poses the question: 'There are more than 20,000 Colonial people who live among us. What do we know of them – of their work, of their living conditions, their hopes and grievances? Picture Post conducts a survey into this dangerous and important question.'
The figure is refined further:

Although there are no official figures, the coloured population of Great Britain is estimated by both the Colonial Office and the League of Coloured People at about 25,000, including students. This total is distributed over the whole of Britain, but there are two large concentrated communities: one of about 7,000 in the dock area of Cardiff round Loudon Square, popularly known as 'Tiger Bay', and the other of about 8,000 in the shabby mid-nineteenth century residential South End of Liverpool …Smaller coloured communities are found in all the main ports, including London (there is one of about 2,000 in North and South Shields), in Manchester and the industrial areas of the Midlands.

Passing the time on the corner
of Upper Parliament Street and
Princes Road. (Not published)

IS THERE A BRITISH COLOUR BAR ?

Photographed by BERT HARDY

Britain stages Colonial Month—a campaign to stimulate popular interest in the life and people of the Colonies. The King attends the opening ceremony. But there are more than 30,000 Colonial people who live among us. What do we know of them—of their work, of their living conditions, their hopes and grievances? Picture Post conducts a survey into this dangerous and important question.

On the Curb of a Liverpool Pavement a Coloured British Subject Expresses the Indignation of His People

Unestablished Seamen Sit Hoping for a Ship in a Seaman's Pool Canteen

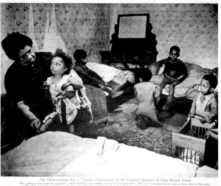

The Overcrowding that is Typical of Conditions in the Coloured Quarters of Some British Towns

The Stowaway Sees His Dreams Begin to Crumble

Two Men Happy At Their Work. The Paper Baler

And the Student of Medicine

White and Coloured Share a Problem

A Marriage That Can Lead to Difficulties

Social Segregation That Can Lead to Trouble

Half a Pint That Can Only Lead to Friendship

The immigrant community is described as covering people from more than fifty colonies, mainly Somalis, Adenese Arabs and West Indians. A distinction is made of the 3,500 students studying in Britain. They are described as the 'aristocrats of the coloured community', with many relying on private means and a third on scholarships. Although they are recognised in the article as being relatively well-off, in comparison to other compatriots, their living conditions in hostels are described as generally poor and depressing. This raises the crux of the article:

But more important – because less material – student grievances bring one nearer the heart of Britain's colour problem. In principle, coloured students dislike living in hostels. They come to England because they have admired England and English life from a distance, and want to know it from close to. But they cannot do that if they live in hostels full of their own people. Why then do they stay there? The answer is distressingly simple: because it is often very difficult for any coloured man – student or not – to find a furnished flat or room in England. Even the Colonial Office often has difficulty in placing a coloured man in lodgings.

The overcrowding that is typical of conditions in the coloured quarters of some British towns. Mrs Johnson lives with her two daughters, whose husbands are seamen, and eleven grandchildren. She and six grandchildren sleep in three beds in this room: Mrs Johnson and two children in the bed, top right, three children in the bed on the left, and an older grand-daughter in the bed in the foreground. (Picture Post caption)

Where society knows no colour prejudice: Liverpool schoolchildren at play. On the roof of the Windsor Street County School, in the South End of Liverpool, white and coloured children play naturally together. They attach no meaning to differences in colour. A white and coloured child will often be 'best friends.' From such children, society can learn a valuable lesson. (Picture Post caption)

Suitcase in hand, a new arrival looking for accommodation on Upper Parliament Street. (Not published)

This is the 'colour bar', an unofficial and pernicious racism that was prevalent wherever the immigrant groups tried to establish themselves.

The operation of this particular unofficial colour bar is almost always the same. A coloured man, perhaps with a name like Smith or Murdoch, will write or ring up in answer to an advertisement and be told to call to see the room at a certain time. The landlady, when she sees him, will usually say quite politely that the room has just been let. In many cases a check carried out by a white friend immediately afterwards will prove that the room is still available. From a social survey made just before the Second World War, it was estimated that up to 60 per cent of landladies, boarding-house keepers and private families in England would refuse to take a coloured person into their homes. Most landladies explain their attitude in a manner characteristic of English colour prejudice in general: "I wouldn't mind for myself. But there's no telling what the other lodgers might say."

…But a more important difficulty still, because it relates to the general social problem, is the initial reluctance shown on all sides to welcome coloured workers. The coloured man meets prejudice in connection with his employment from all classes. It may come from an ignorant Ministry of Labour clerk, who will be reluctant to submit a coloured man for a job. It may come from a reactionary employer who states categorically that he will not employ coloured labour, or from an employer, who, like the landlady, says he doesn't mind himself but he doesn't like to risk the effect it may have on other workers. Very often, in fact, it will come from the white workers themselves.

The coloured worker arriving in this country with many illusions will find that he has not only to deal with a different labour situation from that which he anticipated, but also a threefold prejudice (social, in housing, and in employment). It is not surprising that if he meets with these in a particularly virulent form he himself turns bitter and fills with prejudice. He will forget, if he lives in a slum, that there are white people who live in one too. He will see the whole social system as a conspiracy against his colour.

Interestingly, apart from the population statistic, Liverpool is only mentioned once is the body of the article: 'One of the most permanent and symbolic obstacles to peace is perhaps the existence of segregated communities. The close coloured communities of Cardiff and Liverpool may give a sense of defensive security to the coloured people who live in them'. The direct references are in the photographs that accompany the article, the majority of which were taken in the city by photographer Bert Hardy. The article ends, perhaps, on a predictable note, that racism can 'be solved by a true integration of white and coloured people in one society. And for that to take place there must be some sort of revolution inside every individual mind – coloured and white – where prejudices based on bitterness, ignorance or patronage have been established'. Not exactly a radical solution, but, sixty years on, are we any nearer to finding solutions with an infinitely greater immigrant population?

Social segregation that can lead to trouble. In many big towns, coloured people live together in close communities. In such communities grievances are brooded on more bitterly. (Picture Post caption)

The stowaway sees his dreams begin to crumble. He stowed away from Lagos to realise his dream of working in the 'Mother Country.' The police gave him Service clothing, the Colonial Office gave him temporary lodging, the Assistance Board gave him £2 a week. But no one in Liverpool can give him a job. The danger is that he may drift. (Picture Post caption)

North v South
for the Cup

Up North they're unimpressed with Arsenal's team of
stars. Of course they're good, but they believe that their
own all-round side, eight of which cost nothing, will prove
themselves better in the Cup Final at Wembley on Saturday.
But London's faith is pinned on as sturdy a defence as
football can show, and forwards who may not look much
on paper, but who rather like their chances of setting the
Mersey on fire.

Published 29 April 1950
Photographed by William Vanderson

The left-half who scored in the Semi-Final. Bob Paisley clears near the goalmouth against Burnley. A Durham man, he came to Liverpool without transfer fee from Bishop Auckland. He scored the first goal against Everton. (Picture Post caption)

Football featured regularly in the pages of Picture Post and the added excitement of a Cup Final was always an easy piece to fit into the week's schedule. Liverpool had been First Division champions in 1946/47 and Arsenal had taken the honours the following year, so there was no shortage of interest in the outcome.

The article followed the usual pattern of journalistic sitting on the fence, with supporting grainy photographs of the key players. One photograph, in particular, catches the eye – that of a young Bob Paisley clearing his line. The Final finished with an Arsenal victory (2-0). Sadly for Bob, the Cup Final was the only major trophy that eluded him as a player and manager.

Housewives scrubbing their front doorsteps. A
memorable image and one of the most striking
John Chillingworth took on this assignment.
(Not published)

The Best and Worst of British Cities

Published 3 April 1954
Written by Brian Dowling
Photographed by John Chillingworth

Ferry commuters taking their rather bizarre constitutional on the deck. (Not published)

In 1954, Picture Post decided to look at a number of British cities, starting with Liverpool:

Liverpool is a city on its own. It is a cosmopolitan city, spread out like an open fan on seven miles of docks. It has its own humour – the humour of Tommy Handley. It has its accent – the language of 'Scouse', compounded in equal parts of Irish and Welsh and catarrh. You can lean on the wind that blows in from the Irish Sea, driving scraps of paper before it. Gulls wheel overhead. The sirens sound on the river. Salt water runs in its veins.

The River Mersey has always been Liverpool's greatness. And in times like the 'thirties, when one man in four was unemployed, it has also been her sorrow. Directly, or indirectly, it touches on all the city's affairs. It explains the growth and life of her well-mixed population, and the pattern of her commerce and industry. It explains

why Liverpool became a pioneer in planned industrial development – to counteract the mercurial effect of world trade, whose booms and slumps are felt more early in Liverpool than anywhere else in Britain.

It is Britain's second biggest port, as big as the next eight put together, and it handles more export trade than London. It grew on coal and salt (you will still see the salt-sellers, with their horse-drawn carts in the streets); on privateering, smuggling and the slave trade; on traffic with the East and West in molasses and spices, tobacco and cotton and wool, raw material for her own and Britain's industries. It was the capital port of the Western Approaches, and some Liverpudlians complain that Britain, who thought so much of her then, has less thought to spare for her now.

The coloured population of Liverpool would fill a sizeable town. It is about 30,000. The races are from all over the world – but many are born and bred in the city. There are problems, of course. But they are common to all Britain. (Picture Post caption)

The article examines Liverpool's history: the enormous population growth in the 1840s, particularly from Irish immigration, but the main thrust is of its post-1945 economy:

The Port, and all the services connected with it, is still the biggest business, employing 17 per cent of the Merseyside working population. But 19 per cent of the Merseyside working population is engaged in some sort of manufacture now. Next to the Port, come chemicals and pharmaceuticals; then light engineering; then food and foodstuffs production.

The Port, and food production, are traditional industries in Liverpool. But it is significant that the other two, the second and third biggest industries, are new to the city on any large scale.

There never has been overwhelming prosperity since the days of the merchants who gave the city her big black buildings. However, the balance is now being struck between production and distribution. The city could face another slump considerably better; and it is not expecting a slump.

AS SEEN FROM THE SHIPS OR FERRIES, LIVERPOOL IS DOMINATED BY THE PIER-HEAD BUILDINGS

THE BEST AND WORST OF BRITISH CITIES: OUR NEW SERIES STARTS WITH

LIVERPOOL

Photographed by JOHN CHILLINGWORTH
Written by BRIAN DOWLING

UNDERNEATH THE FERRY—the Mersey Tunnel connects Liverpool with Birkenhead.

LIVERPOOL IS BRITAIN'S SECOND PORT, bigger than the next eight put together.

THE CITY OF THE SEA

THE COLOURED POPULATION of Liverpool would fill a sizeable town.

THE IMAM ALI HIZZAM, spiritual leader of Liverpool's 2,000 Moslems.

MR. H. TYSON SMITH, the sculptor, is a representative of Liverpool's strong and individual culture.

SPORT AND BETTING employ tens of thousands of Merseyside working women.

THE CITY POLICE is in constant manufacturing industry.

THE SEAMEN OF TODAY are more civilian-minded.

THE TOWN HALL is the centre of civic life.

THE DOCKS are lined with warehouses.

CHEMICALS and pharmaceuticals are the second industry of Liverpool.

50,000 PEOPLE work here.

The conclusion, though, is somewhat downbeat. Liverpool had a future, but its best days were behind it.

This is, at best, a sketch. The essence of Liverpool is not easily distilled. It has a sad look of glory gone to seed; a tattered tradition of 'Manchester men, Liverpool gentlemen'; of merchant princes overshadowed by manufacturers. The balance of its future will be more weighed down by industry. People may think of it as a label on a machine or an address on a pools coupon. But whatever industry does, it will be freshened by the wind off the sea. The office workers from 'over the water' - from Wallasey, Seacombe and Birkenhead - will go on tramping the ferry decks on their solemn constitutional, like prisoners at exercise. Citizens will go on knowing the times of the tides, the sounds of the ships' sirens. The great Pierhead buildings - the Cunard, the Dock Office, the Liver Building, with its clock faces bigger than Big Ben's, and its golden liver bird which ought to be a cormorant - will symbolise the city to anyone who ever sees it. The best, and the worst, of Liverpool arises from the sea.

Unquestionably, Liverpool was going through a deep cycle of decline and it would be wrong to deny the prevailing sense of despair that permeates the article. Perhaps the best response came from a Liverpool headmaster in a published letter three weeks later:

Brian Dowling, writing about Liverpool on 24 April 1954, says: This is at best, a sketch. It would be truer to call it a caricature, for although he calls it 'The Best and Worst', he emphasises the uglier points and practically omits the better features of the city.

He draws in hard black lines the alien element, the crime problems, unemployment and gambling figures, but he does not show us the real cultural life of Liverpool, the tremendous loyalty of its ordinary folk, the political and religious vigour, the transport - Speke airport and the railway termini - or our sports activities, to
mention but a few points worth elaborating.

Pools coupon checking at Littlewoods. (Not published)

A mother and children peering out of a window at a new housing estate at Kirkby. An earlier photograph in the sequence was published with the caption: '58,000 people want houses. Progress is good. On two estates at Kirkby alone, 30 or 40 are built every week'. (Not published)

Assembly at a secondary school. (Not published)

A young boy playing with a chain outside his family home. (Not published)

Admiring a bike.
(Not published)

Not published.

Not published.

Who needs toys when you have a
gutter to play in? (Not published)

Picture Post did not have a monopoly on the
best photographs. Other magazines had to raise
their standards to compete and this dynamic
photograph by John Pratt of the Keystone agency,
in 1958, captures Bessie Braddock in a truly
memorable pose.

Battling
Bessie Braddock

*Mrs Elizabeth Margaret Braddock, JP, Councillor
for Central Ward and Member of Parliament for the
Exchange Division of Liverpool, is a turbulent character
even in a city where passions run high. People love her,
and people hate her; but nobody can disregard her.*

*Published 20 November 1954
Written by Brian Dowling
Photographed by Bert Hardy*

Mrs Braddock buckles down
to it. She is governed by a
woman's common sense,
(Picture Post caption)

The name Bessie Braddock probably means little to the under-40s, a sign perhaps that most politicians only have a short time in the spotlight. Bessie fared better than most and for much of the 1950s, her doughty figure wading into action made the front pages of most national newspapers and magazines. 'Battling Bessie', as the media loved to call her, epitomised the firebrand Socialist standing up against injustice. Mention her name and the world became polarised as Picture Post reported:

One Saturday, a lady told us, "Don't talk to me about that woman! She's a disgrace! She's a scandal!" And on that same Saturday, we saw a little inked legend in the waiting room outside the office where Mrs Braddock receives her constituents. It simply said, 'God Bless Our Bess'.

She has a great gift of indignation. She wades into her battles like the boxers whom she so much admires, goaded by the slightest idea of injustice or under-privilege.

The Exchange Division is very much a cross-section of Liverpool, embracing the University, the two Cathedrals and a large coloured population. It has main thoroughfares, and streets where grass springs up through the cobbles. Mrs Braddock prides herself on her accessibility. As she drives or walks around, running three conversations at once, she stops - or is stopped - all the time. "There's nobody'" she says, "however poorly dressed, that won't come up to me. And the same with children - even the tiny ones."

Bessie Braddock talking
to one of her constituents.
(Not published)

The article is sympathetic. Here is an MP with real empathy for her constituents, a woman who will stand up and fight for a better, more equal society.

She took us in her car (it isn't a very small car, but she makes it seem so) to the redevelopment area around Page Street, in her Council ward and constituency. The street turned out to meet her. There are houses there without sanitation of any kind; houses where families with ten children have two bedrooms. Mrs Braddock asked a few questions, made a few notes, and said that she was doing what she could. She didn't show soft sympathy: "Sympathy is fatal," she says. "Just show a little of it, and they keep you at it all day, when you ought to be doing something about it." But her wrath was growing visible, and soon she blew up.

"People say I'm a bully," she said, "…and coarse and crude, and all that. But look at it! Look at it! LOOK AT IT!" Housing like this was the subject of her maiden speech, and she spoke true to form. *"In industrial areas,"* she said, in 1945, *"our people are living in flea-ridden, bug-ridden, rat-ridden, lousy hell-holes."*

She arrives at her office on Saturday morning, for interviews with constituents. No one is ever turned away. If she can help, she does. If she can't, she says so. (Picture Post caption)

BATTLING
BESSIE BRADDOCK

Written by BRIAN DOWLING   Photographed by BERT HARDY

Mrs. Elizabeth Margaret Braddock, JP, Councillor for Central Ward and Member of Parliament for the Exchange Division of Liverpool, is a turbulent character even in a city where passions run high. People love her, and people hate her; but nobody can disregard her.

MRS. BRADDOCK LOOKS IN ON A SLUM IN HER WARD WHICH IS DUE FOR CLEARANCE.

SHE ARRIVES AT HER OFFICE ON SATURDAY MORNING, FOR INTERVIEWS WITH CONSTITUENTS.

MRS. BRADDOCK BUCKLES DOWN TO IT. SHE IS GOVERNED BY A WOMAN'S COMMON SENSE.

BESSIE GETS DOWN TO HER HOMEWORK

THE ONE WHO DOES THE TALKING. Mrs. Braddock makes a speech.

A Juvenile Liaison Officer keeps an eye on his boys. (Not published)

When a Boy's Best Friend is a Policeman

The Liverpool Police started a Juvenile Liaison Scheme, which is a model for Britain. In five years, it has set more than two thousand offenders on the right path.

Published 4 December 1954
Written by Brian Dowling
Photographed by Bert Hardy

The Juvenile Liaison Scheme was started in 1949 by Chief Constable Mr CC Martin. Nine plain-clothes policemen and women (one for each division) visited homes, schools and youth clubs getting to know the youths of their areas:

A few weeks ago, a popular newspaper carried the headline: 'Novel Police Plan Cuts Child Crime'. It quoted an address by the new Home Secretary, in which he praised the Liverpool experiment of Juvenile Liaison Officers. The headline, Liverpool thought, was a little behind the times. The plan was really novel five years ago; today it is a settled part of the city's life.

Yet let us admit that it isn't a headline-catcher. It doesn't work with patrol cars and short-wave radio, or round up murderers and mail-bag robbers. It concerns itself solely with children: children who break street lamps or filch bars of chocolate from the big stores, or children who look as if they might.

The majority of their charges, however, are young people who have been cautioned by the police for committing a minor first offence. If this sounds unimportant, remember that these nine people have looked after 2,350 cases in four-and-a-half years – and only one in ten of these children has committed a second offence. The year before the scheme started, forty-one in a hundred first offenders were booked a second time. This year, the figure is six. And in one Division alone, there are between thirty-five and forty thousand children.

The scheme was heralded as a great success. Shopkeepers welcomed the drop in pilfering and teachers noted a two-thirds drop in delinquency. But, in Picture Post's concluding paragraph:

The greatest testimonial came from an old lag, who had spent a great deal of time in Walton Gaol. He went up to the JLO one day. "Look here, copper," he said, "I don't like the company my boy's mixing with. Just keep an eye on him, will you? I don't want him to turn out like me."

Led by Bob and Alf Pearson, the company at the
Shakespeare drinks a toast. (Picture Post caption)

A Grand
Old Music Hall

The Shakespeare, Liverpool's oldest theatre, is a living museum of music hall. In the face of expensive big stars and cheap nude shows, it manages to keep a home for the traditional 'family entertainment'.

Published 25 December 1954
Written by Brian Dowling
Photographed by Bert Hardy

In December 1954, Picture Post took a nostalgic look at one of the last surviving variety theatres in Britain. The Shakespeare, on Fraser Street, was a magnificent Victorian theatre:

…built, in 1888, by a timber merchant who believed in his stock-in-trade. There is hardly a nail or a piece of iron in the building; everywhere it is wood and polished brass, and red plush, and every available inch is moulded or painted, ornamented or carved. Nobody could build a place like that now. It is out of date, magnificently.

Over its more than 60 years, many of the greats of music hall trod its boards, including Vesta Tilley, Harry Lauder, Will Fyffe, George Formby, senior, Wee Georgie Wood and Lupino Lane. The theatre had enjoyed a post-war boom after three other theatres – the Lyric, Rotunda and Metropole, Bootle – were bombed. The new clientele brought with them their own tradition and 'some of them brought the tomatoes with which they used to make their criticisms felt. But (manager) Peter Jackson sorted that out.'

The final paragraph suggests that, perhaps, the Shakespeare's days were numbered:

Now and again, when it is not possible to fill a variety bill, a nude show creeps in, but that is not in the Shakespeare's tradition. It may do good business, but it frightens off the family trade. And the Shakespeare's tradition is a fine one, not to be lost: an antidote to the big stars, big theatres and big prices that dominate variety today.

Soon after, in 1957, the Shakespeare was taken over by Sam Wanamaker, an American film director, actor, and one-time member of the Communist Party, who had been blacklisted by Hollywood during the McCarthy witch-hunts. The Shakespeare had a short-lived life as an art centre, with plays, films and other activities, before funding ran out. Wanamaker (the father of Zoey) was later instrumental in the recreation of Shakespeare's Globe theatre in London. Liverpool's Shakespeare had a further life as a nightclub before it was destroyed by fire in 1976.

Often, the most striking images were left out of
the published feature. Here, an elderly theatre-
goer, wrapped up against the chill, watches the
performance from the circle. (Not published)

'When it is not possible to fill a variety bill, a
nude show creeps in.' The sign in the background
implores 'Keep Your Act Clean.' (Not published)

Sunday morning in the Cathedral. The people of the city come to worship. "The citizens of Liverpool are rightly proud of their Cathedral," writes the Archbishop of York. They showed their pride by raising more than two million pounds. Even now, when there are hopes that industry and trade will share the burden of completing the cathedral, the shillings and sixpences will still be needed. (Picture Post caption)

Visions of a Cathedral

Two generations have so far helped to build the three million pound Anglican Cathedral in Liverpool. Now a third generation takes over.

Published 4 June 1955
Written by George Eglin
Photographed by Alex Dellow

The man who planned a cathedral planned his tomb there

The building of Liverpool Cathedral was a truly astonishing achievement – a 75-year project to erect a Gothic cathedral in the twentieth century. In the words of Picture Post:

The cathedral is the finest and the greatest built in Britain since Henry VIII destroyed the monasteries. Almost certainly, it will be the last great Anglican cathedral.

The cathedral, built to last at least two thousand years, puts to shame those who have said the time for building great churches is long since past; that the twentieth century, with all its expensive materials and labour, cannot afford to do what the Middle Ages could do with its masons, who earned three pence a day, and its labourers who only asked threehalfpence.

The cathedral builders' answer to that is that in relation to the cost of wages and material prices, the burden to the community of building a cathedral is no greater today than it was in the fourteenth century. The builders have proved their point, too. More than two-thirds of the cathedral is completed. It is thirty years since an appeal for money was made. Yet the building fund is not one penny in debt.

The tempo of work has varied according to the money available. That is why there are only nine stonemasons working today, when, in 1939, there were a hundred and twenty. The principle laid down in 1901, that the cathedral must not be built at the expense of existing Church and philanthropic work, has been strictly maintained.

In twenty years, the Liverpool Cathedral will be completed. Behind it stand faded Georgian terraces. In front, from St James's Mount to the Mersey, are some of the city's slums. Children play almost on the threshold. Yet the humble setting of the greatest Anglican church in the country is a fitting one. For it is truly a church of the people, whose money and efforts helped to build it as much as did the handsome cheques of merchant princes. (Picture Post caption)

This dramatic photograph of stonemasons at work was one of a sequence which failed to make the final feature.

A teenager going nowhere:
one of Liverpool's unemployed
youths sits out another day.
(Picture Post caption)

The Truth about Teenagers

There are the teenagers. Today they are the young people who suck sticky brown stuff through straws, stay out too late, wear the wrong clothes, and think they know it all. But tomorrow, for better or worse, they will be Britain. This is the first part of a series, on what teenagers are and what they hope for.

15 March 1957
Written by Trevor Philpott
Photographed by Bert Hardy

Of all the features about Liverpool, the two-part series about teenagers was the most negative. In fact it was in three parts but the final episode entitled 'Those Wild, Wild Girls' did not include any teenagers from the city.

The actual text of the article starts with an account of the seemingly successful Great Barr comprehensive school in Birmingham but the eye is then taken to the main photograph of a young man lounging on his bed. 'A teenager going nowhere: one of Liverpool's unemployed youths, sits out another day'. The tone is set by the opening paragraph:

We started this inquiry by visiting, in turn, three very different places, to see how the surroundings affected the growth and development of young people. The first was a large area of modern housing estates where the building of houses had far outpaced the building of any communal facilities. The second was an area of overcrowded city dwellings, cramped homes and massive tenement blocks. And the third was the place where most teenagers would like the chance to live – in Cambridge University.

Having nothing but praise for the Great Barr experiment, Trevor Philpott turns his critical eye northwards:

But come to Liverpool where things are rather different. And meet Harry. He's on probation. He is 16 and unemployed. He's been unemployed for the best part of a year now. In the Liverpool area he's not alone in this. At a meeting for unemployed youths at the Liverpool YMCA, 350 turned up. They were mainly like Harry – builders' labourers, who had been stood off at the end of a completed job. Day after day Harry hangs around the street corners or tries to find some little job to do around the YMCA Red Triangle Boys Club, so that he can stay inside in the warm.

His home is enough to make your throat shrink with pity and disgust. On the morning we went there his mother was in. "I've got no 'eart to do anything anymore. No 'eart to do anything." It is gruesomely obvious. All

the way up the stairs the laths are grinning through the crumbling plaster; the bare boards are eaten through, the moisture is seeping down. In the bathroom tiled walls and the ceiling have fallen in. There is no kitchen.

Harry has gone upstairs and is sitting on his bed. There is no mattress and no blankets, just a broken wire frame and a heap of old coats. The springs on both this and his brother's bed are broken and the blackened mattress on the other bed sags on to the floor. From the fireplace the charred remains of some kind of bonfire spread out over the floor. There are three pairs of trousers in the far corner and that's all. The boy at school, it seems, can have only the clothes he is wearing. The two girls sleep in the other room with Mum and Dad.

Harry doesn't talk about his parents' failings or their quarrels. He would probably leave if it were not for the three younger children. In this area it is boys like Harry who are so often 'in trouble'. Here the gang is the normal teenage group. And the gang mustn't think you soft. All girls are spoken to like street-walkers. You mustn't show affection and you mustn't show enthusiasm. No word is too foul, no physical experience is too coarse. What can an unemployed boy do to show what a big fellow he is, when his parents don't give a damn whether he's in the warm or out in the cold, hungry or satisfied, roaming the streets or behind bars?

Well, he can 'nick' a car from outside a cinema, drive it to New Brighton and try to get it back into the garage before the owner comes out. Or he can drive a hearse away as the bearers go in to get the coffin, or he can insult a girl walking by with her boyfriend and help to beat the boy up when he turns round angry and over bold. Oh, there are a lot of things a teenager, without much capital and living in the Everton Road area, can do to prove that he is really going to be the devil of a man.

Boys meet girls in a Liverpool street. Yes, the social graces have changed a little. No time now for many of the formalities of courtship. (Picture Post caption)

So what is the solution? Philpott has the answer:

To get an environment as different as possible from that of the Liverpool back streets we went to Cambridge. Here, amid slow beauty and rich tradition the young student is really given the breathing space to discover himself and to try to learn in what manner he should spend his life in order to find it most worth living. Here, if anywhere, he can discover and develop his talents; here there is no lack of adult people who are taking a sincere interest in his wellbeing. He has a tutor and a director of studies who are deeply concerned both with his academic progress and with his development as a University personality. Here he can indulge in every sport from croquet and lacrosse to rowing and beagling. Here he can indulge his mind in everything from politics to the black arts.

The last paragraph provides an ironic conclusion:

Emigration is a much-used word in Cambridge today. When the Canadian Immigration authorities organised a meeting some weeks ago, over six hundred students attended, nearly one in ten of the University population. Now air-trips are being organised for the long vacation, so that undergraduates can go and 'take a look'. It's a disturbing thought that Cambridge is so much concerned with emigration, whilst the rougher parts of Liverpool are not thinking about it at all.

It would seem that Trevor Philpott is hoping for a mass emigration of those teenagers without a future, but they already tried that out a century earlier, with forcible transportation to Australia! Ironically, in 1949, Picture Post had published a gushing article entitled 'One Glorious Week' about May Week in Cambridge.

If you have the slightest doubt as to whether life is worth living, or youth what it used to be, or if you fear that the pleasures of the exclusive few are destroyed by becoming the pleasures of the many, try Cambridge in May Week … One party (on this scale) had everything, including a fight in the host's rooms that ruined a radiogram. There was also the requisite amount of falling in the river and scaling college portals and towers throughout the week. Those in authority responded with the requisite amount of tolerance. The Master of Clare (College) looked down benignly while his charges, ecstatically burning a boat to celebrate going 'Head of the River' for the first time, shoved a splendid new gardener's wagon on the fire.

"I think the men are behaving themselves very well," he was heard to murmur.

So the line is drawn. What is borderline criminality and devilry in Liverpool, is just boisterous good fun in Cambridge.

The Truth about Teenagers 2.

The ones who live only for tonight.

22 March 1957
Written by Trevor Philpott
Photographed by Bert Hardy

If the first part of 'The Truth about Teenagers' was hard on Liverpool's youth, the second part was not prepared to give them any respite. The tone is overwhelmingly Christian, introducing the young parson who is 'trying to bring his God into the lives of the boys and girls of this blackened, run-down district. They don't want to know, but he keeps telling them just the same.' The sub-heading said it all: 'The boys without a future'. At the Red Triangle Boys' Club, it was time for prayers, a prayer for protection against idleness:

For in this area the Devil, in the shape of a gang leader, will find plenty of work for idle hands to do. And there is plenty of idleness here. In this district there is a good deal of unemployment… Among the teenagers of Britain these are the dead-end kids; the aimless ones; the ones who are most likely to find themselves making the headlines in the newspapers for some rather stupid and badly-planned crime.

One of these out-of-work boys brought in a cup of tea. The club leader waited till the boy was out of earshot. "You'd never think it to look at him, would you? Six months ago he buttered a bloke up properly and ditched him half-conscious into the reservoir…

The next day we went to the boy's house. His mother's hair hung down in greasy snakes over her back and she looked completely defeated and spiritless. The boy and his brother slept under old coats in a filthy, bare-boarded and bare-windowed room…

It is monotony like this out of which street gangs grow and on which they flourish. There are scores of them in Liverpool. Monotony, squalid rooms or broken homes, quarrelling parents, an arrogant father, or one who doesn't give a damn – these are the chief causes for the loungers on the street corners. Alone a boy may feel exposed as a failure, weak and not very brave. But in the gang he is 'somebody'. The gang is tough and dangerous. The gang is something which nobody laughs at.

The article continues in this tone. Stealing cars, even a hearse outside a house while the bearers were fetching a coffin. As for girls: 'Sooner or later the boys will find themselves with time on their hands, a dark place – and her.' The parson was a patient man: 'You have to wait for the crash, for the showdown. Then you get a chance to turn them into Christians.'

Coffee party in the West
Derby Road, Liverpool.
The dance hall has just
closed. The café is about
to close. From then on the
night is wide open. (Picture
Post caption)

The family in Myrtle Gardens. Dado (right) is the eldest of the boys left at home and the chief breadwinner. His mother has
eight surviving children. His father, suffering from crippling asthma, has not worked for six years. They live on the fourth
floor of a massive council tenement. (Picture Post caption)

By way of contrast, this photograph was published in the third part of 'The Truth about Teenagers – Those Wild, Wild Girls'. Captioned 'Afternoon on the River under the willows of Trinity College', it projects the ideal of young people working for their (and the country's) future.

This photograph of girls at Girton College, Cambridge, enjoying crumpets and tea was not published, although the magazine makes the rather improbable claim that 'The girl in the next room at Girton College may quite well be the daughter of a postman, or a publican or a professional footballer.'

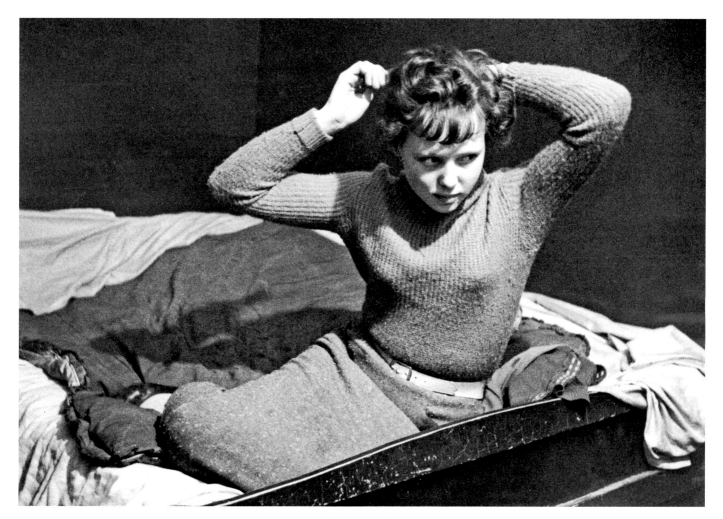

A typical teenage girl in a Liverpool tenement gets ready for her nightly relaxation – a rock 'n' roll session at the local dance hall. (Picture Post caption)

Lime Street Station.

Unpublished Photographs

Most magazines stockpile features that can be fitted in at the last minute if space is available. Sometimes a good idea suddenly seems less interesting in the face of breaking news. Sometimes the photographs might appear interesting but the storyline is considered too weak.

For the photographer on assignment, particularly when away from London, time could be used creatively, seeking out interesting subjects that might be turned later into an article.

Bert Hardy, in particular, was highly productive on his Liverpool visits and he took many more photographs than appeared on the pages of Picture Post. His contact sheets have putative titles: Punch and Judy (the Codman family who plied their trade outside St George's Hall), Lime Street (as essay on a busy mainline railway station), Mersey Ferries and, the most politically sensitive, photographs of a hostel for Chinese merchant sailors.

Bert Hardy (1913-1995) was a self-taught photographer who had left school at 14 to work for a chemist who processed photographs. Fascinated by photography, he freelanced for The Bicycle magazine and bought a small-format Leica camera. He started work for Picture Post in 1941 and quickly established himself with his images of London in the Blitz. He worked for the Army Film and Photographic Unit during the War, taking part in the D-Day Landings, the Liberation of Paris, as well as being one of the first photographers to enter Belsen concentration camp.

Speakers' Corner at Pierhead.

Mersey Ferry.

Chinese Merchant Seamen

Amongst the most politically sensitive photographs taken in Liverpool were those of Chinese merchant seamen. Liverpool had a long-standing Chinese community, dating back to the nineteenth century and centred round Pitt Street. The community had been in slow decline, but the onset of war in 1939 had reinvigorated it, as up to 20,000 seamen were based in the city.

From the start, there were serious issues. The basic pay for a British seamen was over £12 but the Chinese were only getting a maximum of £5 15s for working in conditions that were deemed 'not really suitable for white crews'.

As the War progressed, casualties mounted and, by September 1940, over 100 Chinese seamen had been killed on British ships, with no compensation for their families. Unsurprisingly, desertions and requests for repatriation increased significantly. As the situation worsened, disputes over working conditions led to those involved being imprisoned and deported, provoking a collective sense of grievance amongst the Chinese, which remained unabated for the duration of the War.

However, the fall of Singapore and Hong Kong to the Japanese removed the option of deportation and, under growing pressure, an agreement was signed in London, in 1942,

that gave additional remuneration, including a £10 a month War Risk payment. Shortly after, this move to close the wages gap was undermined when British seamen were offered a further increase in pay that was denied to the Chinese.

Desertions continued to rise significantly as seamen refused to accept the low pay and bad treatment. As the War ended, matters came to a head again as the War Risk Bonus was removed (but not from British seamen, in contradiction of the 1942 London Agreement). The subsequent action taken to deport a majority of the seamen after the War, even though hundreds had married British women, is a sad episode in the history of racism in Britain.

There is a later strand to the story. The photographs taken by Bert Hardy in 1942 relate to the negotiations leading to the London agreement. They are strong, moody images of men on shore leave, passing their time in Liverpool hostels. The images were never published and it is likely that Bert Hardy knew the Censor would never agree to such damaging photographs appearing at a time of national crisis. Fortunately, the negatives survived and a dark episode of colonial history was captured for posterity.

Passing time in the hostel.

The hostel's basic facilities did not stretch to a bathroom.

The Slums of Liverpool

1956: Unpublished
Photography by Thurston Hopkins

The best photographic essay on Liverpool was never published by Picture Post. The actual circumstances are somewhat difficult to pin down but it appears that Edward Hulton, the proprietor of the magazine, was pressured by members of Liverpool City Council to drop the feature, which they felt was a slur on the city. For whatever reason, Hulton acquiesced and Fyfe Robertson's article, along with Hopkins' photographs, was spiked.

The text for the feature appears to have been lost but it is clear that Fyfe Robertson was forthright about the failures of those in power to tackle the endemic poverty in a large part of Liverpool. Fortunately, Thurston Hopkins' stunning photographic essay has survived in its entirety and 23 of the images are reproduced here.

There was an ironic development to the story. The following year, a selection of the photographs won the prestigious Encyclopaedia Britannica Prize for photo-journalism. The British Journal of Photography reported:

It will be remembered that last year there was a remarkable sequence by Jack Esten, of Picture Post, on the Hungarian revolt - a set of pictures taken under difficult circumstances and which set a new high in camera journalism. This year's winning sequence by Thurston Hopkins is equally as good, in fact I am not sure that in some respects it does not excel the 1965 winner.

Here we have a set of 22 pictures of commonplace scenes: scenes which might possibly - in fact almost surely - be duplicated in a number of our great cities. They are pictures of everyday life; of men, women and children fighting for existence, struggling to maintain the comforts of home life and striving to retain some of the dignity of humankind under conditions which are appalling and which cannot

Two boys showing off
the latest in modern
conveniences.

What would Jamie Oliver or Nigella Lawson make of this 1950s kitchen?

be realised by many millions whose lot has been cast in happier surroundings.

Thurston Hopkins has lifted a stone in our much-vaunted Welfare State and shown, with unemotional clarity, some of the things that people would prefer not to see or know about. Here is superb photography - stark in its realism; an example of photographic journalism at its very best. The pictures tell their own story, carry their own message, and while being a damning indictment of the City Fathers of Liverpool, are perfect examples of how it is possible to weld the trained eye of the cameraman to modern photographic technique in order that a civic conscience might be aroused. This sequence is the high spot of the 1957 Encyclopaedia Britannica exhibition, and should be seen and carefully studied by all photographers, whether amateur or professional.

Remarkably, Thurston Hopkins, who began his career in Fleet Street in 1930, is still active (as a painter now) at the age of 98. Fifty-five years after the events of that 1956 assignment, he expressed strong feelings about the suppression of the feature and his photographs in a letter to me:
To answer your 'big question': why were my pictures of Liverpool in the 50s never published in Picture Post, I enclose, to begin with, a photocopy of The British Journal of Photography's (BJP) comment on the affair. No, sorry, I've just seen that there is no mention in the highly flattering piece of the fact that the feature did not appear in the magazine which commissioned it - or rather sent two staff members to carry it out. Fyfe Robertson (my future father-in-law) was the writer, with me, on the job, a relentlessly thorough man who, no doubt, put quite a few backs up.

Curious that the BJP made no comment on the fact that the photographs never appeared in Picture Post and only acted when they appeared in the annual show of press photography, some time after they were scheduled to be published in the magazine. Today even the photographic press would make something of the shady business, linking it with the scandal surrounding Bert's (Bert Hardy) coverage of the Korea war, which resulted in the sacking of PP's great editor, Tom Hopkinson.

Today the real villain behind both of these 'incidents', the magazine's snobbish proprietor, Edward Hulton, would be quickly exposed. It was Robbie (Fyfe Robertson) who told me that the feature was killed on Hulton's order, because he did not want to get wrong with Liverpool's City Fathers for social reasons. The real laugh is it was The Amateur Photographer, which published a limited, but well-presented selection of my images later on!

My memory of that week roving around the city's really bad spots is of encountering friendliness and hospitality almost everywhere. As soon as we uttered the words "Picture Post", doors flew open, a cuppa was produced

A typical slum with no bathroom: just a basin of warm water in the kitchen to wash in.

A despairing mother surveys her dismal surroundings.

The old woman in an alley who reminded Thurston Hopkins of a Rembrandt portrait.

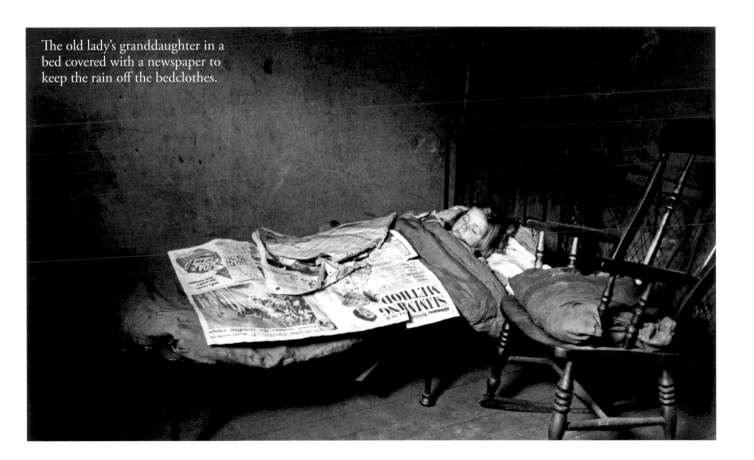

The old lady's granddaughter in a bed covered with a newspaper to keep the rain off the bedclothes.

and reminiscences of years of living in the area flowed. There was bitterness with conditions, and anger that so little had been done to improve them, but the moans quickly developed into laughter and joking about their raw deal. Robbie's sympathetic questioning was rewarded with advice where we should go next for conditions much worse than those I was busy photographing.

I don't think I ever saw the contact sheets of the Liverpool story. So often you were shot off to another job before you had a chance to go through the work you had just handed in for processing and editing, but one series of pictures sticks in my mind because the most striking shots have often been reproduced and written about. I expect you are already familiar with the splendid old lady, with a face which makes you think about Rembrandt, emerging from a narrow passage. After I photographed her at various stages of her descent, I told her what we were doing – Robbie wasn't with me that morning, he was probably grilling

some unfortunate town Councillor. Anyway, after we had chatted for a few minutes, the old lady said: "Oh, you really should see where my daughter's little girl has to sleep" and she made me write down the address, which I had some difficulty finding in such a generally let down area.

As you can imagine, I've often been suspected of having introduced the badly soiled newspaper covering the child's bed, and I've often wondered if I shouldn't have removed it before taking the photo, or even first photographed it without the child in it, which I may well have done during my wait for her to get back from school. I asked the mother if she had nothing else to keep the child warm when asleep and she pointed out to me that rainwater dripped through the faulty overhead skylight and she found that newspapers which could be changed daily was the best way of keeping bedding dry. Well … so when the child obediently slipped beneath the covers and, like the little actress she was, closed her eyes as if she had really dropped off after a

By the hearth.

hard day at school, I did not have the feeling that I was photographing a rigged picture. I'd no doubt that this was how it was, night after night. (A publication abroad said the picture of the child in bed was like a glimpse of Charles Dickens. Right!)

Hulton's action in refusing to publish what would have been a controversial feature on the 'failure' of the Welfare State is still difficult to understand. As a staunch, though eccentric, Conservative, it is surprising to see him rush to support a Labour Council. Thurston Hopkins asserts that this was about social rather than political connections, and maybe that was the case. From a contemporary standpoint, one can understand Liverpool City Council wishing to suppress yet another negative piece about the city's notorious slums. Their argument probably ran along the line of why us again? Find another town, another slum.

There is validity in their stance but, in this particular case, the work was too important to be discarded for the sake of a council's misplaced honour. There is no pride in having so many people living 'Dickensian' lives. The job of investigative journalism is to expose such conditions and bring them to the notice of a wider public.

Hopkins' reference to the controversial sacking of Tom Hopkinson over Hulton's similar stance concerning photographs showing the brutal mistreatment of North Korean captives during the Korean War indicates his anger over the proprietor's inability to allow editorial judgement to take its due course. The ultimate failure of Picture Post was in no small measure due to such dilution in the power of the editor, resulting in a whimsical and capricious policy that gradually sucked out all magazine's energy.

What we are left with is a powerful collection of images that appear even more shocking today. Did people really live like that just fifty years ago? We know they did and we know the camera is true. The articles on teenagers in Britain were largely fatuous, tainted with a middle-class perspective of what is 'nice'. The photographs were largely there to support a particular 'Christian' viewpoint. The 'Slums of Liverpool' photographs are of a different nature. They say, unambiguously:

These are living conditions which everyone should be ashamed of. What is being done to eradicate such poverty? Half a century later, the tragedy is that the same question is still being asked.

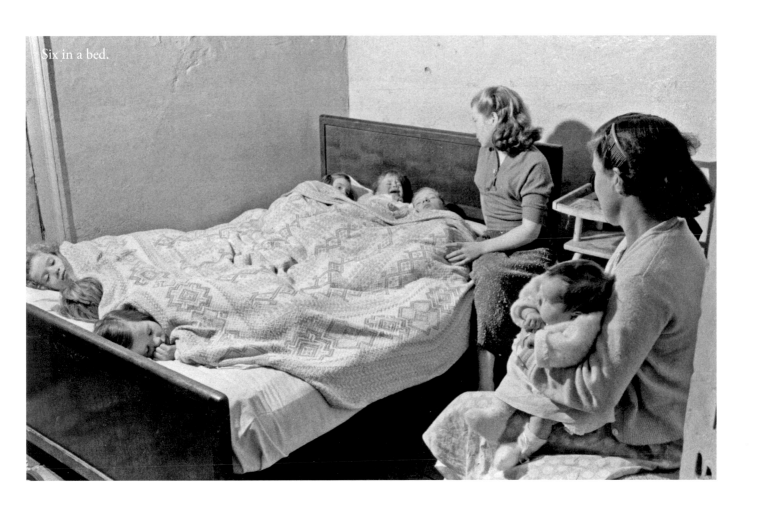

Six in a bed.

At the bar.

The landlady (right) with some of her regulars.

Paddy's Market.

In the picture of the harassed father carrying his baby son, I was too occupied with obtaining any kind of exposure in the dim light to be really aware of the other children dancing around him. To me the edge of darkness is a magical time; black and white film might have been invented to serve the nocturnal imagination. "Black, far more than all the resplendent colours of palette and prism, is the medium of the mind," wrote the painter Odilon Redon, and it really does seem that black and white, much more than colour photography, has the power to sort out and emphasise significant form. (I remember revelling in the bad light prevailing throughout the slums.)

Thurston Hopkins